THE BANTAM LIBRARY
of Culinary Arts

Jams & PRESERVES

JILL NORMAN

BANTAM BOOKS
TORONTO · NEW YORK · LONDON · SYDNEY · AUCKLAND

JAMS & PRESERVES

A BANTAM BOOK/PUBLISHED BY ARRANGEMENT WITH
DORLING KINDERSLEY LIMITED

PRINTING HISTORY
DORLING KINDERSLEY EDITION
PUBLISHED IN GREAT BRITAIN IN 1989

BANTAM EDITION/MAY 1990

EDITOR GWEN EDMONDS
DESIGNER MATTHEWSON BULL
PHOTOGRAPHER DAVE KING

ART DIRECTOR STUART JACKMAN

LIBRARY OF CONGRESS CATALOGING-IN-PUBLICATION DATA

NORMAN, JILL.
JAMS & PRESERVES.
DELICIOUS RECIPES FOR JAMS, JELLIES, AND SWEET PRESERVES /
JILL NORMAN. — BANTAM ED.
P. CM. — (THE BANTAM LIBRARY OF CULINARY ARTS)
"DORLING KINDERSLEY EDITION PUBLISHED IN GREAT BRITAIN 1989" — T.P. VERSO
INCLUDES INDEX.
ISBN 0—553—05737—5
I. JAM. I. TITLE. II. TITLE: JAMS AND PRESERVES. III. SERIES
TX612.J3N67 1990
641.8'52—DC20
89—6866   CIP

PRINTED AND BOUND IN HONG KONG
0 9 8 7 6 5 4 3 2 1

C O N T E N T S

4
INTRODUCTION

6
APPLE, PEAR &
QUINCE

8
CITRUS
FRUITS

10
CHERRIES

11
CRANBERRIES

12
DRIED FRUITS

14
NUTS

16
PLUMS

18
SOFT FRUITS

20
STONE FRUITS

22
WILD FRUITS

24
RECIPES

40
INDEX

INTRODUCTION

"The rule is jam tomorrow and jam yesterday – but never jam today."

Lewis Carroll, Alice Through The Looking Glass

Date box, c. 1930

THE WHITE QUEEN'S "VERY GOOD JAM" *would certainly have been home-made. Making jams and preserves was for centuries an important part of the domestic economy, as the profusion of early recipes indicates. It was the province of the lady of the house and her maids who gathered fruits from the garden during the summer months and preserved them.*

Cherries, apricots, quinces, raspberries and red currants were among the most popular fruits, cultivated widely in the gardens of the well-to-do. With the arrival, by the later part of Elizabeth I's reign, of cheaper sugar from the colonies the making of fruit jellies, pastes and marmalades spread to more households and eventually became a commercial proposition, as well.

Sir Kenelm Digby offers several versions of quince paste and a delicious recipe for raspberry jelly with whole red currants. "It will look like rubies in clear gelly," he said (The Closet Opened, 1669) *– and indeed it does.*

The English may well have learned to make quince and other pastes from the Spanish or the Portuguese, who are still renowned for this confection. They in turn had most likely learned the art from the Moors, for the making of jams and sweetmeats has a long history in the Middle East. In The Thousand and One Nights you can read of sumptuous conserves, jams and crystallized fruits that were offered to guests. Such preserves might, then as now, be flavored with spices – cloves, coriander and cardamom.

In the days of the Ottoman empire there was often close contact between Jewish women and those of the harem, and many Turkish dishes, particularly sweets, were adopted by the Jews. At the end of the Sabbath it became customary among the Jews of the eastern Mediterranean to offer small bowls of special jams – quince or rose petal or date – to their guests, who would take a spoonful of jam and then a sip of water. In Turkish households the visitor may still be welcomed with this same ritual.

French jam label, c. 1908

I have chosen recipes from east and west, past and present that conserve the flavors of one season for another. All are for fruits preserved with sugar, and occasionally with vinegar and alcohol. Who can resist the clean fruit flavor of homemade marmalade, the unmistakable scent and delicate color of rose petal jam or an after dinner treat of mellow fruits in brandy?

APPLE, PEAR, QUINCE

*A*PPLES AND QUINCES *are excellent fruits for making preserves. They contain a high level of pectin, which means the fruit will set easily when cooked with sugar. The bland taste of cooked apple makes it useful to mix with low pectin fruits without altering the flavor. Pears are low in both pectin and acidity and so are usually combined with fruits like cranberry or boosted by lemon juice when making preserves.*

Pear

APPLES are the most important and the most widely grown fruit of the temperate zones, and in the northern hemisphere they have been cultivated for 4,000 years. One of the most versatile fruits.

PEARS grow in many temperate and subtropical zones. The eating pear with its "melting" flesh was created after A.D. 1500; cooking pears, with harder "granular" flesh, were cultivated earlier.

QUINCES are shaped like pears or apples but are more irregular; the skin is golden yellow with a gray downy covering. Cultivated in ancient Greece, they still come mostly from the Mediterranean.

Apple

Quince

CITRUS FRUIT

*C*ITRUS FRUITS *flourish in most tropical and subtropical regions, a "citrus belt" that stretches between latitudes 40 degrees north and south. The small trees probably originated in China and South-east Asia and were cultivated both for their valuable fruit and for decorative purposes.*

ORANGES come in two varieties: the common sweet ones with orange flesh and juice (the red-fleshed kind is even sweeter) and the bitter Seville oranges grown mostly for marmalade.

LIMES, as acidic as lemons but more fragrant, can be used much as lemons are but do impart an intense flavor of their own. They grow only in the citrus belt's tropical zones.

Lime

LEMONS are the subtropical *alter ego* of limes. Too acid to be eaten fresh, they nevertheless offer an enormous variety of culinary uses.

GRAPEFRUITS are a West Indian hybrid of the pomelo, which had reached the West in the 12th century. The yellow to pink flesh has a pleasant balance between sweetness and acidity.

Seville orange

Grapefruit

Lemon

CHERRIES

HERRIES are cultivated in all temperate zones but their region of origin remains unknown. The aromatic, sweet and juicy fruit is a "one-seeded drupe", that is, it has a stone at its center. The trees are large with a profusion of attractive white flowers in spring to produce a summer fruit that can be yellow, red or very dark purple and that grows in clusters on long individual stalks.

The northern and very hardy bird cherries are used to flavor rum and brandy.

The sour, or morello, cherries of dark fruit and flesh are mostly grown in south-eastern Europe, where they have become the basis for a wide range of products – from Black Forest gâteau to the famous eau-de-vie, Kirschwasser.

Cherries

CRANBERRIES

*C*RANBERRIES *grow wild throughout Western Europe, northern Asia and North America as an evergreen prostrate shrub with dark and oblong leaves. The small pink flowers give way to equally small pale yellow berries, which ripen to deep red and become a cheerful but very tart winter fruit that keeps remarkably well. Its natural habitat, marsh and bogland, may well account for its Old English name of fenberry.*

The larger cultivated cranberry is grown only in North America. It, too, is tart (especially the skin), but when fully ripe it can be eaten fresh, whereas the wild cranberries are only used cooked, to make sauces and preserves.

Cranberries

DRIED FRUITS

*D*RIED FRUIT *is very different in taste and texture from the fresh original. Dehydration produces a much greater concentration of flavor as well as a much higher sugar content. Most of the dried fruit available commercially comes from hot climates. Dried fruits should be added toward the end when making a preserve to keep some of their texture.*

Date

DATES, the shiny brown fruit of the date palm which grows in many dry sub-tropical regions, taste of honey, but are slightly tart, with a fibrous texture. Semi-dried they are very sweet but still juicy.

Prune

PRUNES are dried on the tree in hot climates. Best are the French prunes d'Agen with a high fructose level. They are usually available in three sizes. Most commercial prunes come from California.

Apricot

APRICOTS, unlike dates or prunes, have the stone removed before they are dried; they can also be found as a dried paste, usually in the form of sheets, with different culinary possibilities.

Fig

FIGS vary in color from deep purple to yellowish green. They are sweet, nutty and crunchy; sometimes a little tart. Figs should be thick and springy; light-colored ones are usually best.

NUTS

Nuts are autumn fruits consisting of an edible, usually hard and somewhat oily kernel within a hard or brittle shell. The ones shown here are all natives of the temperate climates in the northern hemisphere. They have been gathered as food since prehistoric times, and many have long been cultivated to be eaten fresh, roasted or salted, processed for their oil, preserved by candying or pickling, or ground into flour.

Hazelnut

HAZELNUTS, or cobs, are native to Europe and North America. Their cultivation on a large scale did not begin until the 19th century.

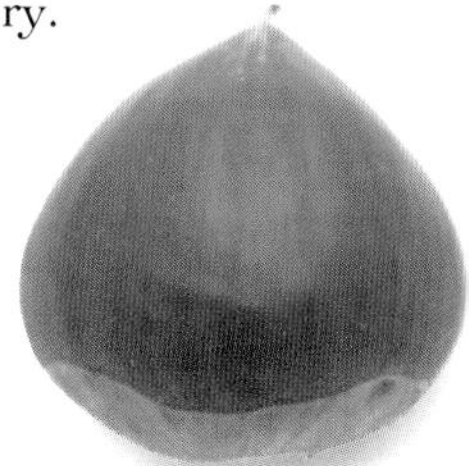

Chestnut

Filbert

CHESTNUTS grow two or three at a time in green spiny cupules. The pith is bitter and needs to be removed; the nut itself becomes sweet and soft when roasted.

FILBERTS belong to the hazelnut family. Their husks are longer than the nut, while those of hazels are short and round. Confusingly, the best known of the filberts is the "Kentish cob."

ALMONDS have long been cultivated and are now grown successfully in the northern and southern hemispheres. They are probably the most widely used nuts, and they certainly have the largest share of world trade.

Almond

Green almond

GREEN ALMONDS are the new fruit, with a husk that is fibrous and not yet hard. The bitter almond is a mildly poisonous variety, valuable as the source of culinary and cosmetic almond oil.

WALNUTS are different in the Old and New Worlds, the European ones being smaller but considered better than the American black walnut.

Wet walnut

Walnut

"WET" WALNUTS are a delicacy of the new harvest. Even earlier, unformed green fruit is picked for preserving in brine or syrup, or used in salads.

PLUMS

*P*LUMS, *the hardiest of the stone fruits,*
range from the small golden
mirabelle and the many gages to
the large commercial varieties (such as victoria),
which are hybrids of the wild sloe and cherry plum.
They should always be plump, fully
colored and fresh in appearance.

Greengages

GREENGAGES are known on the
Continent as reine-claude (after
the wife of Francis I [1494–
1547] during whose reign they
were created). They were
introduced into England about
1724 by Sir Thomas Gage. Soft,
honey-sweet and juicy, they are
the ideal all-purpose plum.

VICTORIA PLUMS are one of the many varieties developed by deliberate breeding during the latter part of the 19th century. Their ability to withstand a certain amount of cold storage has made them one of the most heavily commercialized sorts.

Damsons

Victoria plums

DAMSONS, which can still be found in the wild, have an intense, tart but sweet flavor. They have firm flesh and are not very juicy, which makes them good for cooking purposes.

SOFT FRUITS

S OFT FRUITS *have long been the natural choice for a great variety of preserves. Their season is so short and they are so universally enjoyed that their use out of season stimulates the imagination as much as the appetite: we feel again the warmth of summer and smell, in jams and jellies, fruit liqueurs and syrups, the fragrant fruit ripening on the bush. All the soft fruits of summer are perishable and fragile, so extra care must be taken when picking or buying them.*

Strawberries

Blueberries

STRAWBERRIES: small wild strawberries are prized for their fragrant fruit. The large cultivated fruit originated in America and came to Europe in the 17th century.

RASPBERRIES are a compound fruit with many small drupelets around a conical core, and are native throughout the northern hemisphere. Yellow raspberries have an excellent flavor.

Raspberries

CURRANTS (red, black or white) grow wild in all of Europe, in bunches close to a stalk. The sharp and very pippy reds are cultivated farther north than the sweeter but tangy blacks.

Red currants

BLUEBERRIES belong to the same family as blackberries, whortleberries and bilberries. Small, blue-black berries, with purple flesh and often acid juice, they are used mostly in cooking, but ripe blueberries are good to eat.

Black currants

STONE FRUITS

S TONE FRUITS, *so called because the thin-skinned and juicy fruit encloses a single "stone," or seed, all belong to the genus* Prunus, *which embraces cherries and plums as well as apricots and peaches. These deciduous trees are hardy in all temperate climates, cherries and plums farther north than apricots and peaches. The latter need warmer weather and are only really satisfactory when tree-ripened – in which state they travel badly and are hard to find in the shops.*

Nectarines

NECTARINES are a hardier, firmer and more aromatic variety of peach, with smooth skins. They grow in temperate and subtropical parts of Europe and North America.

APRICOTS were cultivated in China at least 4000 years ago and now grow in many subtropical regions. Fibrous, not overjuicy, tart but also sweet, they find a wide variety of uses.

Peaches

Apricots

PEACHES are pale to deep yellow, but a crimson blush gives their downy skin, with its pronounced seam, a much deeper glow. Their flesh is sometimes rather fibrous; when fully ripe they are juicy, succulent and sweetly aromatic.

WILD FRUITS

WILD FRUITS *grow all around us in great abundance matched by almost complete neglect. Rosehip, sloe, crab apple, rowan, hawthorn: the names may evoke memories, but more of tales than of experience. Even elderberries are more talked about than used, and perhaps only blackberries can be said to have been gathered by all. In an age when food is increasingly being altered to suit commercial interest, wild fruits can be a reminder of what taste once was.*

Blackberries

BLACKBERRIES, or brambles, compounds of small fruitlets around a fibrous hull, are native everywhere in the northern hemisphere. The wild berry is more tart than the cultivated – it may require more sugar for some purposes, but makes a better jelly.

Elderberries

Bilberries

Wild plums

WILD PLUMS are all smaller than
the cultivated varieties. Usually
rather tart and with a high stone-
to-flesh ratio, few can be eaten fresh.
The cherry plum, darker bullace, and
acid sloe all have their special appeal.

ELDERBERRIES grow
in umbels with unusually
long individual stalks. They
have a rather cloying taste,
but the unpleasantly
astringent aftertaste
disappears when they are
cooked. In jams and
jellies they combine well
with other fruit.

Recipes

CHERRY JAM

This jam can be made with dark
sweet cherries or morellos.

2 lb/1 kg cherries
1½ lb/750 g sugar
juice of ½ lemon
2 oz/50 g chopped walnuts
(optional)

Remove the cherry pits, put the cherries and their juice in a large heavy non-reactive pot and tie a few of the pits in a cheesecloth bag. Add the bag to the pan and simmer for 3–4 minutes, then put in the sugar and stir until it dissolves. Bring to the boil, stirring frequently, then cook until the fruit is soft, about 15 minutes. Add a little water if necessary to prevent it sticking to the pan. Discard the bag of stones and stir in the lemon juice. Bring to the boil again until sheeting stage is reached (105°C, 220°F). Remove any scum, stir in the walnuts if you wish, and put the jam into warm clean jars. Attach lids when cold.

AUTUMN FRUITS JAM

1 lb/500 g apples or crabapples
1 lb/500 g blackberries
1 lb/500 g elderberries
1 lb/500 g bilberries or blueberries
4 oz/125 g hazelnuts
¼ teaspoon ground cloves
2½ pints/1.5 liters water
4 lb/2 kg sugar

Peel, core and chop the apples;
rinse the berries and remove
leaves and stalks. Chop or
process the nuts to a coarse
powder. Put the fruit, nuts and
cloves in a heavy pot with
the water and simmer until the
fruit is soft, about 15 minutes.
Add the sugar and stir until it
dissolves then bring to the boil
and continue to boil, stirring
from time to time, for
about 10 minutes,
until sheeting stage is
reached. Remove
any scum, pot
and cover
while still hot.

STRAWBERRY JAM

3½ lb/1.75 kg strawberries
3 lb/1.5 kg sugar
juice of 1 lemon

Wash the strawberries, then
hull them. Put a layer of sugar in
the heavy pot, then a layer
of strawberries. Make more
layers, finishing with a layer of
sugar. Let stand for 24
hours. Bring the pan gently to
the boil, and when all the sugar
has dissolved boil steadily for
12–15 minutes. Add the lemon
juice, test for setting, then cool
slightly and pour into jars.
This jam has an excellent
flavor, but will not keep
for more than 4–5
months.

*R*OSE PETAL JAM

A delicacy throughout the Middle East, this jam must be made with richly scented, preferably red or pink, roses. Few modern roses are suitable for making jam; the gallicas, which, despite their name, originated in Persia, make the best jam, particularly *officinalis*, the Apothecary's rose. It has a delicate fragrance and color and an exquisite taste.

"*Ghyulbè-Shèkèr.*—When the roses are in full bloom, gather about a *pound of the leaves* (*petals*), pick out the large ones, and cut the white ends off with a pair of scissors; then put the small ones and the white ends in a very clean stewpan with *three-quarters of a pint of water*, and scald them; then pass the liquor through a piece of cheesecloth or a sieve, squeeze well the leaves and throw them away; then put the liquor in the pan with *three and a half pounds of white sifted sugar*, and stir them with a wooden spoon till the sugar is dissolved; then add the large leaves that you have picked out, stir and boil till rather thick, or try a little on a plate. If it sets, then remove it from the fire. When cold, fill the preserve jars, cover them airtight, and keep them in a rather cool place."

Turkish Cookery Book, A collection of recipes compiled by Turabi Effendi, 1862

It takes about 10 minutes for the jam to thicken and the juice of a lemon helps to set it.

26

CHESTNUT JAM

"Boil the *chestnuts*, peel them
and crush them through a wire
sieve. Make a syrup of *three-
quarters of a pound of sugar* to each
pound of chestnuts, and flavor it
well with *vanilla*. Add *half a glass
of water.* *

When the syrup is ready throw
in the purée, and cook till fairly
stiff. It ought not to be too stiff;
there ought with this jam to be a
certain amount of syrup.
Pour into pots."
Mrs C. F. Leyel, *The Complete
Jam Cupboard*, c. 1925

*Use ²/₃ cup/150 ml water to each
1¾ cup/375 g sugar

GREENGAGE JAM

*4 lb/2 kg greengage plums
2½ lb/1.25 kg sugar
juice of 1 lemon*

Cut the plums
in half and remove
the stones. Put the fruit and
sugar in a bowl and let
stand for several hours.
Turn the mixture into a
heavy pot and bring
slowly to the boil. Add the lemon
juice and cook until sheeting
stage is reached. Pot and cover.

RASPBERRY AND ROSE GERANIUM JAM

*4 lb/2 kg raspberries
4–5 rose geranium leaves
²/₃ cup/150 ml red currant juice
4 lb/2 kg sugar*

Put the fruit, leaves and juice in
a heavy pot and cook for
10 minutes until the fruit is soft.
Warm the sugar in a low oven,
tip it into the pan, bring quickly
to the boil and boil vigorously
for 3 minutes. This jam does not
set to a very firm consistency,
but it has an excellent flavor.
Remove the leaves before
pouring into jars.

CREOLE JAM

"One of my favorites. Because of its alcohol content it is definitely not for breakfast, but is excellent served at the end of a meal with *fromage blanc*.

3 lb (1.5 kg) bananas
2 lb (1 kg) superfine sugar
1¼ cups (300 ml) water
2 large lemons or 3 limes
½ teaspoon ground cinnamon
⅔ cup (150 ml) rum

Peel the bananas, cut into slices and blanch in boiling water for 1 minute. Drain. Prepare a syrup with the sugar and 1 cup (250 ml) of water. Add the bananas and cook for 25 minutes. Meanwhile peel the lemons or limes, taking care to leave the pith on the fruit. Cut the zest into thin shreds (scissors are best for this) and blanch for 2 minutes. Drain. Squeeze the lemons or limes and add their juice to the bananas with the zest and cinnamon. Let thicken for 15 minutes more, stirring from time to time. Take off the heat, pour in the rum, mix well and put into jars."

One of my favorites too. This recipe is from *Particular Delights* by Nathalie Hambro, 1981.

SPICED BLACKBERRY JELLY

3 lb/1.5 kg blackberries
1¼ cups/300 ml water
¼ teaspoon ground mace
¼ teaspoon ground cinnamon
pinch of ground cloves
sugar
juice of 2 lemons

Put the blackberries, water and spices in a heavy pot. Bring to the boil and simmer for 30 minutes or until all the juice is extracted. Stir and press the fruit occasionally. Strain through a jelly bag. Measure the juice and for each pint/600 ml add 1 lb/500 g sugar. Put the juice, sugar and lemon juice into a heavy pot and cook gently until sheeting stage is reached, then pot.

DRIED APRICOT AND ALMOND JAM

1 lb/500 g dried apricots
6¼ cups/1.5 liters water
juice of 2 lemons
grated rind of 1 lemon
2 lb/1 kg sugar
2 oz/50 g blanched almonds, split

Soak the apricots overnight in the water. Drain the fruit, reserving the liquid and chop coarsely. Chop the almonds. Put the apricots, soaking water, lemon juice and rind into a heavy pot and simmer for 20 minutes, stirring from time to time.

Add the sugar and almonds and stir until the sugar has dissolved. Then boil rapidly, stirring frequently to prevent the jam from sticking, until sheeting stage is reached, about 10–15 minutes. Pot and cover.

NECTARINE JAM

2 lb/1 kg ripe nectarines
2 lb/1 kg sugar
1¼ cups/300 ml water
juice of 1 lemon
10 cardamom pods, cracked

Pour boiling water over the nectarines to loosen the skins. Peel them, cut in quarters and remove the pits. Put the stones and cardamoms in a cheesecloth bag. Bring the sugar and water to the boil, add the lemon juice and the cheesecloth bag and then the fruit. Bring to the boil again, and simmer gently for 30 minutes.

If the jam will not set, discard the cheesecloth bag, transfer the fruit with a slotted spoon to the jars and boil the syrup until it does set. Skim and cool, then pour over the fruit and cover.

CRANBERRY JELLY

"Wash and pick the cranberries, put them in the preserving kettle with a very small quantity of water, cover closely and stew till done. Pour through a jelly bag or coarse towel, without squeezing, as this will prevent it from being clear. Measure and pour the liquid into the preserving kettle. Let it boil up and remove the scum, then add the sugar, cut or loaf,* one pound to a pint. Boil about twenty minutes, or until it jellies. It preserves the color of fruit jellies to add the sugar as late as possible."

Housekeeping in Old Virginia,
ed. Marion Cabell Tyree, 1879

* Use granulated sugar.

GRAPEFRUIT, LEMON AND GINGER MARMALADE

2 grapefruit
2 lemons
3 lb/1.5 kg sugar
11½ cups/2.7 liters water
5 oz/150 g crystallized ginger, chopped

Wash the fruit, remove the peel and cut in thin strips. Remove the pith, including the pithy centers of the grapefruit. Cut the fruit into thin slices. Put the seeds and some of the pith in a cheesecloth bag and put the bag into a heavy pot with the peel and fruit. Pour over the water and simmer for 1½ hours. The contents of the pan should have reduced by almost half. Remove the bag and squeeze it well. Warm the sugar and add to the pan. Stir until it dissolves, then bring to a fast boil, stir in the ginger and cook until sheeting stage is reached. Let cool for 10 minutes, stir to distribute the peel and ginger through the marmalade.

SEVILLE ORANGE MARMALADE

3 lb/1.5 kg Seville oranges
sugar

Wash the fruit, put it in a casserole, cover with boiling water, then cover and cook in a low oven, 160°C, 325°F, for 3–4 hours until the fruit is soft. Take the oranges out of the casserole and reserve the liquid. Cut up the fruit, removing the seeds. Put the seeds into the cooking liquid and boil for a few minutes. Strain.

Weigh the fruit pulp, and for every pound/500 g take 1½ lb/ 750 g sugar and ¾ pint/450 ml liquid. Put everything into the heavy pot, and cook gently until the sugar has dissolved, then boil rapidly until sheeting stage is reached – about 10 minutes. Skim and let the marmalade cool slightly before putting into jars.

LEMON CURD

1¼ cups/250 g sugar
3 oz/75 g butter
grated rind and juice of 3 lemons
3 eggs

Put all the ingredients except the eggs in the top of a double boiler or in a bowl placed over a pan of simmering water. When the butter has melted, whisk the eggs and stir them in. Stir constantly until the mixture thickens – it will take 10–15 minutes. Do not let the mixture boil or it will curdle.

Pot and cover, and when cold store in the refrigerator where it will keep for about a month.

GREEN WALNUT PRESERVE

This recipe comes from Greece. It is rather time consuming but well worth making if you have a supply of green walnuts.

2 lb/1 kg green walnuts
2 lb/1 kg sugar
4 cups/1 liter water
juice of 3 lemons
6 cloves

Wear rubber gloves while preparing the walnuts or your hands will be badly stained. Peel off the outer skin – a potato peeler works well – and soak the nuts in a large bowl of cold water for 6–7 days, changing the water twice a day. This will draw off any bitterness.

In a stainless steel or enameled pan boil the sugar, water and lemon juice together to make a thick syrup. Drain the nuts and add them with the cloves. Simmer for 40 minutes, remove from the heat and let cool.

Make sure the nuts are submerged in the syrup – put a plate on top if necessary – and leave for 48 hours. Then bring the syrup to the boil again and simmer for a further 40 minutes. Pour into warm preserving jars, cool and close. The nuts are served in a small bowl with a little of the syrup, usually accompanied by a glass of water.

RED CURRANT CONSERVE

A mixture of white and red currants can be used if you wish.

2 lb/1 kg red currants
3 lb/1.5 kg sugar

Strip the currants from the stalks. Dissolve the sugar in 1½ pints/900 ml water. Boil the syrup until it registers 250°F on a sugar thermometer or when a little syrup dropped into iced water forms a ball. Add the currants and boil for 2 minutes. Remove the pan from the heat and let cool for half an hour. Pour the conserve into jars, distributing the fruit evenly. Keep pushing the currants down until they no longer float to the top, then cover the jars.

PEAR PRESERVE

3 lb/1.5 kg ripe pears
8 oz/250 g pineapple
a small piece of cinnamon
juice and grated rind of 1 lime
2½ lb/1.25 kg sugar

Peel and chop the pears,
discarding the core and seeds.
Put them into a heavy pot
with the pineapple and the
cinnamon tied in a cheesecloth
bag. Simmer for 20 minutes
then stir in the lime juice and
rind and the sugar. Bring to the
boil, then lower the heat and
cook slowly for a further 20
minutes, stirring frequently.
Remove the
cinnamon and pot the preserve.

QUINCE PASTE

4 lb/2 kg quinces
juice of 1 lemon
sugar

Wipe the quinces to remove their downy coating, but do not peel. Cut them in quarters and then eighths and put them in a heavy pan with the lemon juice and water to cover. Cover the pan and simmer until the fruit is soft – about 30–40 minutes.

Drain and press the fruit through a sieve to purée it. Weigh the purée and for each pound/500 g take the same weight, or slightly less, of sugar. Put the purée into a heavy pot over a very low heat and add the sugar, a little at a time. Stir constantly with a long handled wooden spoon to avoid being burned, because as the paste thickens it erupts and spits. Make sure the paste doesn't stick to the bottom of the pan. It needs to cook for at least an hour, until it thickens so that a spoon drawn across the bottom of the pan leaves a clear path.

Turn the paste into shallow metal trays lined with

waxed paper. Cover with a light cloth and dry thoroughly for 4–5 days in an airing cupboard until the paste has dried completely and is firm to the touch. Then cut into small pieces, dust with superfine sugar and store in an airtight container. Quince paste makes a good after-dinner sweetmeat.

APRICOT PASTE

"Boil some apricots that are full ripe to a pulp, and rub the fine of it through a sieve; to every pound of pulp, take one pound two ounces of fine sugar, beaten to a very fine powder; heat well your paste, and by degrees put in your sugar; when all is in, give it a thorough heat over the fire, taking care not to let it boil; then take it off, and scrape it all to one side of the pan; let it cool a little, then lay it out on plates in what form you please; then put into the stove to dry."
Hannah Glasse, *The Complete Confectioner*, 1800 edition

After the sugar is added stir constantly to prevent sticking – it will take 40 to 50 minutes for the paste to dry sufficiently so that a wooden spoon drawn across the bottom of the pan leaves a clear trail. Put the paste into waxed-paper lined trays.

Dry out for 2–3 days, as described for Quince Paste. When properly dry – cut into small pieces and store in a tin. Semi-dried apricots can be used in place of fresh.

DAMSON CHEESE

A cheese is a thicker version of a fruit butter, made by adding an equal weight of sugar to fruit pulp. It is economical to make cheese with the pulp left in the jelly bag after making jelly. It need only be sieved before using.

Put the *damsons* in a pan with *just enough water* to prevent them from sticking, and simmer until soft. Sieve and weigh the pulp. Weigh an *equal quantity of sugar* and put in a low oven to warm. Return the pulp to the pan, add the sugar, stirring well to dissolve it. Then cook over medium heat, stirring frequently, until the cheese is very thick.

Oil straight-sided wide jars with *almond oil* and put in the cheese. Cover; it will keep for at least 3 months.

Blackberries, gooseberries and apples all make good cheese.

PEACH AND DATE CHUTNEY

6 peaches
4 oz/125 g dates, pitted and chopped
4 oz/125 g raisins
2 onions, chopped finely
12 oz/375 g soft brown sugar
2 cloves garlic, chopped finely
1 tablespoon mustard seeds
2 tablespoons fresh ginger, chopped
finely
6 cardamoms, outer shells removed
2 teaspoons salt
1¼ cups/300 ml tarragon vinegar

Plunge the peaches briefly into boiling water, then remove the skins and pits and slice them. Put all the ingredients into a heavy pot and heat gently until the sugar has dissolved. Bring to the boil, then simmer for 1½ hours, stirring from time to time until the mixture is thick. Pot and store for at least a month before serving.

SHERBET DRINKS

"Sherbets are made of almost all tart pleasing fruits as the juice of pomegranets, lemmons, citrons, oranges, prunellas, which are to be bought in the markets."

A New Account of East India and Persia, Being Nine Years' Travels, 1672–1681
John Fryer, 1698

Sherbets are refreshing summer drinks made with fruit syrups diluted with water and ice. Use a tablespoon of syrup for each glass. The syrups are easy to make, and can also be used as sauces for ice cream and cold desserts. Sealed bottles of syrup will keep at room temperature, but once opened they should be stored in the refrigerator.
When making syrups use an enameled pan and a wooden spoon to avoid discoloration or a metallic taste.

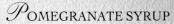

POMEGRANATE SYRUP

pomegranates
sugar

Cut the pomegranates in half
and squeeze out the juice on a
lemon squeezer. Measure the
juice into a pan and add double
the volume of sugar.
Heat gently until the sugar has
dissolved, then boil for a minute
or two until it thickens slightly.
Strain through a cheesecloth-
lined sieve and bottle.
Orange, red or black currant
or mulberry syrup may
be made in the same way.

LEMON SYRUP

3 lb/1.5 kg sugar
3³/4 cups/900 ml water
2 cups/450 ml lemon juice
a few strips of lemon peel

Bring the sugar and water to the
boil, and when the syrup starts
to thicken add the lemon juice
and peel. Simmer for a few more
minutes then strain through a
cheesecloth-lined sieve
and bottle.

CRÈME DE CASSIS

Black currant liqueur is very easy to make at home. Inexpensive, flavorless eau-de-vie from France works well instead of brandy; vodka is also suitable.

2 lb/1 kg black currants
4¼ cups/1 liter brandy or eau-de-vie
1 lb/500 g sugar

Crush the black currants and put them in a large preserving jar. Pour over the brandy, cover and keep in a cool place for at least 2 months. Drain the alcohol from the fruit. Dissolve the sugar in 1¼ cups/300 ml water, and when the syrup is cool add it to the alcohol. Bottle, cork and keep for at least 2 months – the longer you keep it, the mellower the cassis will be. A teaspoon of cassis in a glass of chilled white wine makes a Kir. It also improves black currant ices and puddings.

PRUNES IN RUM

Follow the instructions for Dried Figs in Brandy, using dark rum and prunes.

DRIED FIGS IN BRANDY

Fill a jar with some good *dried figs* and cover with a mixture of *two parts runny honey* to *one part brandy*. Macerate for 2 months before serving.

CHERRIES IN BRANDY

Prick the *cherries* two or three times with a needle and trim the stalks down to ½ in/1 cm. Put a layer of cherries in a preserving jar, sprinkle thickly with *sugar*, then another layer of cherries and more sugar. Continue in this way until the jar is three-quarters full. Fill with *brandy*, cover and leave for 3 months. Serve 2 or 3 cherries in a small glass with a little of the brandy or use as a sauce for ice cream.

PECTIN

The basic setting agent for preserves is pectin, a substance found in all fruit, but for jelling to occur, the balance between acid and fruit must be right. Some fruit such as apples, currants, citrus are high in pectin; most of these fruits have a high acidity as well and so will set easily when cooked with enough sugar. Fruits like cherries, pears, peaches are low in pectin as well as acidity, so both have to be added to make a preserve. The easiest form in which to add acid is lemon juice, while pectin can be increased by combining high and low pectin fruits or by adding commercial pectin.

TESTING FOR SETTING

Test the preserve when it begins to thicken slightly. Take up a little on a wooden spoon, hold it level over the pan for a few seconds, then tilt to pour the preserve back into the pan. If it forms a flake on the edge of the spoon which then falls away slowly, it is ready. Another test is to put a little on a cold saucer and push it with a finger after a few seconds; if it wrinkles it will set. If still runny, boil longer and retest in a few minutes. A reading of 105°C/220°F, on a sugar thermometer indicates the sheeting stage. When ready remove any scum from the surface, stir to distribute the fruit evenly and pot.

POTTING

Scald jars in boiling water and warm in the oven before filling. Cover the preserve with a waxed paper disk, waxed side down, pressed onto the surface, while it is still very hot. Then cover with a transparent disk or a piece of cloth, secured with a rubber band or reuse a twist-on lid. Cover while still very hot or when quite cold, never warm, because this allows moisture to form and causes spoilage. Store chutneys in jars with vinegar-proof lids; glass lidded preserving jars are best.

INDEX

A

Almond, 15
  Green, 15
Apple, 6–7, 25, 35, 39
  Crab, 22, 25
Apricot, 20, 21, 35
  dried, 12–13, 29
  dried, and almond jam, 29
  paste, 35
Autumn fruits jam, 25

B

Bilberry, 19, 23, 25
Blackberry, 19, 22, 25, 35
  jelly, spiced, 28
Black currant, 19, 38, 39
  Crème de cassis, 38
  syrup, 37
Blueberry, 18, 19, 25

C

Cherry, 10, 39
  Bird, 10
  Morello, 10, 24
  in brandy, 38
  jam, 24
Chestnut, 14
  jam, 27
Citrus fruits, 8–9, 39
Crab apple, 22, 25
Cranberry, 11
  jelly, 30
Crème de cassis, 38
Creole jam, 28
Currants, 19, 39 See, black, red and white currants

D

Damson plum, 17
  cheese, 35
Date, dried, 12–13, 36
Dried apricot and almond jam, 29
Dried figs in brandy, 38
Dried fruits, 12–13

E

Elderberry, 22, 23, 25

F

Fig, dried, 12–13, 38
  in brandy, 38
Filbert, 14
Fruits, varieties:
  citrus, 8–9, 39
  dried, 12–13
  soft, 18–19
  stone, 20–21
  wild, 22–23

G

Gooseberry, 35
Grapefruit, 8, 9
  lemon and ginger marmalade, 30
Greengage, 16
  jam, 27
Green walnut preserve, 32

H

Hazelnut, 14

L

Lemon, 8, 9, 39
  curd, 31
  syrup, 37
Lime, 8

M

Mulberry syrup, 37

N

Nectarine, 20
  jam, 29
Nuts, 14–15
  Almonds, 15
  Chestnuts, 14
  Filberts, 14
  Green almonds, 15
  Hazelnuts, 14
  Walnuts, 15
  Wet walnuts, 15
  See under individual varieties for recipes

O

Orange, 8, 9
  syrup, 37
  Seville, 8, 9
    marmalade, 31

P

Peach, 20, 21, 39
  and date chutney, 36
Pear, 6–7, 39
  preserve, 33
Pectin, 39
Plums, 16–17, 20
  Bullace, 23
  Cherry, 23
  Damson, 17
  Greengage, 16
  Mirabelle, 16
  Sloe, 23
  Victoria, 16, 17
  wild, 23
  See under varieties for recipes
Pomegranate syrup, 37
Potting, 39
Prune, dried, 12–13
  in rum, 38

Q

Quince, 6–7
  paste, 34

R

Raspberry, 19
  and rose geranium jam, 27
Red currant, 19, 39
  conserve, 32
  syrup, 37

Rose-hip, 22
Rose petal jam, 26

S

Setting, testing for, 39
Seville orange, 8–9
  marmalade, 31
Sherbet Drinks, 36
Sloe, 22, 23
Soft fruits, 18–19
Stone fruits, 18–19
Strawberry, 18
  jam, 25

Syrups, fruit, 36, 37

V

Victoria plum, 16, 17

W

Walnut, 15
  Wet, 15
  green walnut preserve, 32
White currant, 19, 32, 39
Whortleberry, 19
Wild fruits, 22–23

A C K N O W L E D G M E N T S

*The publishers
would like to thank the following people:*

JACKET
· PHOTOGRAPHY ·
DAVE KING

· TYPESETTING ·
WYVERN
TYPESETTING LTD

· ILLUSTRATOR ·
JANE THOMSON

DESIGN
· ASSISTANCE ·
SUE CORNER

· REPRODUCTION ·
COLOURSCAN
SINGAPORE

PAGE 4-5
RETROGRAPH ARCHIVE
COLLECTION

PAGE 25
SILVER JAM SPOON
COURTESY OF
GERALD SATTIN LTD.
LONDON

PAGE 25
WEMYS WARE PRESERVE POT
COURTESY OF
ROGERS DE RIN.
LONDON

PAGE 31
SILVER-GILT
ENGRAVED SPOON
COURTESY OF
GERALD SATTIN LTD.
LONDON

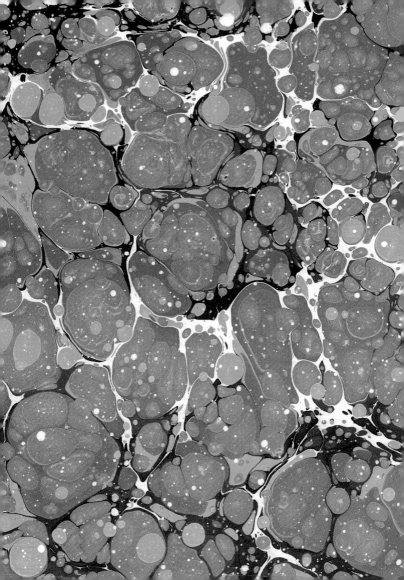